Barcelona

Text, photography, planning and reproduction, entirely conceived and carried out by the GEOCOLOR team

Layout: Eduard Busquets
Translation: Joyce McFarlane
Photographs: C. Socias, J.C. Castañeda, J. Oliva, R. Bristow, S. Gómez, E. Busquets, Y. Fernández.
Acknowledgements to: Museu de Cera de Barcelona and Museu d'Història de Barcelona

Dep. Legal: B-25.531-2012

Introduction

The origins of Barcelona have been traced back as far as the late Neolithic era and the Romans in their day undoubtedly influenced its early development as a city. But it was an Iberian tribe, the Laietani, who first left their unmistakeable mark on the territory, shortly before it was occupied by the troops of Hannibal Barca ('the Great'), from 218 to 202 B.C. So while the exact date of the city's foundation is difficult to establish, most historians opt for the start of Carthaginian rule in the area, 218 B.C.

Others attribute to Hannibal's father, Amilcar, the first official reference to Barcino, or 'Barci Nova' around 230 B.C.

Roman Barcelona

From 218 B.C. to the 1st century B.C. information on the city is sketchy. The invasion of the Iberian Peninsula by the troops of Ancient Rome, then a republic, aimed to counterbalance Carthaginian domination in the area. It soon led to a conquest and occupation that would last until 19 B.C., the year when Augustus Caesar declared the Romans' complete control over the peninsula, and gave the city the name of 'Barcino'. This is also the name under which it appears in Ptolemy's famous world map, in the 2nd century A.D.

As a city of military origin, it was protected by a wall. In the 1st century B.C. this consisted of a simple structure with a few towers, but it had to be strengthened following the first raids by the Franks and Germans from 250 A.D. onwards.

Visigothic Barcelona

In general, relatively little is known of the period of Visi-gothic domination of Barchinona, Barchinonam or Barchinone. However, it seems that the integration of the Visigoths into the customs and life of the Roman and Palaeo-Christian inhabitants was totally peaceful. While in numerical terms,

itants to maintain their Christian customs, although the cathedral was turned into a mosque. Only a small garrison of troops was allowed, and they were kept busy collecting the special taxes charged to non-Muslims, although these were probably lower than in Visigothic times.

Middle Ages to the 19th Century
From the Middle Ages on and more specifically from the early 11th to the 14th centuries, Barcelona became the trading and eco-

the Visigoth population was not large, they controlled the most important bases of power, including the military garrison and the civil authorities. The first Visigoths to settle in the the city were of the Arian religion while its inhabitants were Catholic.

Muslim Barcelona
Muslim power in the city lasted little more than 83 years, but that was enough for it to become known as Barshiluna, Barshaluna, Barguluna, Barchiluna or Madinat.
The Muslims permitted the original inhab-

nomic hub of a territory that included the kingdoms of the former Crown of Aragon (Catalonia, Aragon, Valencia, the Balearic Islands, Roussillon, Sardinia, Naples, Athens and Neopatria in Greece), vying with the ports of Genoa and Venice in importance.

The Modern Age
The city's hosting of the Universal Exposition in 1888 led it to open out new urban areas, and its fame slowly began to spread abroad as the exposition attracted large numbers of foreign visitors.

A second Exposition in 1929 was the stimulus to modernise and urbanise Plaça de Espanya square and the nearby mountain of Montjuïc, reforming buildings that are still used today in the Trade Fair site and building the Palau Nacional (which now houses the National Museum of Modern Art – MNAC) and the Magic Fountain.

The designation of Barcelona as the site of

mopolitan, multicultural, welcoming city, which has managed to conserve its historic roots while assimilating the changes brought by modern times.

One way of getting to know any city is to take some time to explore the districts where ordinary people live, districts which often jealously guard the history of their old stones and maintain intact the charm and flavour of past ages. In Barcelona this is certainly worth while, and there are even guides available to some neighbourhoods to help you out.

the 1992 Olympic Games led to the transformation of the city, with impressive new constructions and the recovery and modernisation of its beaches. All this contributed definitively to the recognition of the city as one of the world's capitals with an international image that few can match. These days, the Catalan capital is a cos-

The Cathedral and the Gothic Quarter

The Gothic Quarter of Barcelona forms part of the district of 'Ciutat Vella' (the old city). It is indeed one of the oldest parts of the city, and the one that preserves intact much of its valuable architecture, starting from the times of Roman rule around old Mount Taber (the present Plaça de San Jaume).

It was not until the 19th century that the structure of the district underwent a significant change, with the conversion of old church cemeteries into public squares and the demolition of most of the city walls.

These days, any stroll through the narrow streets of the Gothic Quarter conveys the image of a city steeped in history but that

Cathedral of Santa Eulália, main façade.

Assortment of musicians in the Gothic Quarter.

Carrer del Bisbe.

does not take itself too seriously. Typical of this is the obvious contrast between the ancient buildings and the young musicians everywhere, enthusiastically demonstrating their abilities on all kinds of instruments.

These young musicians may not have much of a history, unlike the surrounding architecture which has earned its inclusion in this guide. First, the Cathedral of Santa Eulàlia.

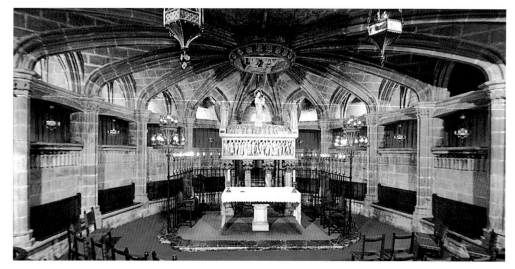

Crypt of Santa Eulàlia.

Main door

Although some historians maintain that there was already a cathedral in Barcelona in the 6th century, the first direct reference to this institution is in 985, when the building was noted as having been destroyed and sacked by the Muslim leader, Almanzor.

In the mid-11th century a new cathedral in Romanesque style was consecrated, but the Gothic building that we see today was not begun until 1298, although the works

High Altar of Barcelona Cathedral.

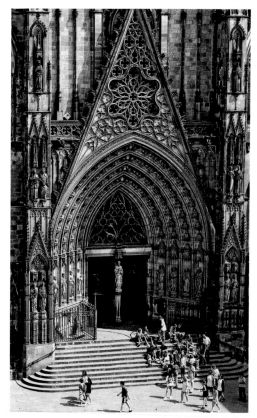

Chapel of Christ of Lepanto.

preserves the remains of the Saint, and over the crypt, the presbytery, with a curious, almost flat vault divided into arches. Her grave, dating from the 14th Century, is sustained by carved alabaster columns.

Next to the High Altar, consecrated in 1337, rises a 15th-century wooden altarpiece.

Outside, the two towers at the end of the transept look symmetrical, but only one houses the 9 bells that the building conserves.

The frontal of the main door of the façade is divided by a figure of the Redeemer and decorated with human figures, angels and prophets. The Door of Sat Iu, the Door of the Pietat, and the Door of Santa Eulàlia provide other accesses to the monument, although the first of these is almost always shut. A further door leads to to the Romanesque chapel of Santa Lúcia, adjacent to the cathedral,

suffered many delays throughout the 14th and 15th centuries, after which they were reinitiated and some progress was made.

However, the construction soon faltered again and was not resumed until the late 19th century, when the International Exposition of 1888 coincided with the inauguration of the main façade of the building. The current basilica consists of three naves with 26 side chapels, the chapel dedicated to the Christ of Lepanto being particularly outstanding. The stone of the High Altar is three metres long and held up by two sturdy capitals from the old Visigothic church.

A central stairway opposite the choir leads down to the Crypt of Santa Eulàlia which

*Door of
Santa Lúcia*

*Door of the Descent
from the Cross.*

Door of Sant Iu.

Detail of interior of the Chapel of Santa Lúcia.

dating from 1268. It preserves two tombs; that of Canon Francesc de Santa Coloma (14th century) and that of Bishop Arnau de Gurb, from the 13th century.

A door inside the nave gives access to the cloister, which can also be reached from Carrer del Bisbe. It has four rectangular galleries leading to several rather soberly decorated chapels and a courtyard where you can observe the peaceful toing and froing of a flock of geese, as well as a beautiful fountain where at Lent you can marvel at the traditional 'l'ou com balla' (dancing egg) .

Barcelona Cathedral has been declared a Historical and Artistic Monument of National Interest.

Earlier we mentioned that the Gothic Quarter is one of the most areas of Barcelona with most monuments per square kilometre. So it will come as no surprise to find yourself almost tripping over one at every turn. Perhaps the nearest to the cathedral is the Casa de l'Ardiaca, opposite the entrance of the Chapel of Santa Lúcia. This 12th-century building is in Gothic style with Italian Renaissance details on some of its figures. One of the motifs that most attracts the eye is the magnificent Modernista letter box in the entrance, with a relief of birds and a tortoise, the work of Domènech i Montaner.

Decorative fountain in the central courtyard of the cloister and details.

Interior courtyard of the Casa de l'Ardiaca. Details of the decoration of the Casa de l'Ardiaca.

At present it houses the Municipal History Archive and the whole building was declared a Cultural Property of National Interest in 1924.

Next to the Casa de l'Ardiaca you will find the Casa Degà, which forms part of the former Roman wall and on the same plot as the Cathedral, the Casa de l'Almoina. Still in the cathedral area and opposite the Door of Sant Iu is the entrance to the

Curious decoration on the letter-box of the Casa de l'Ardiaca with its Modernista motifs.

Frederic Marès Museum, installed in an annex of the southern wing of a palace, the Palau Reial Major.

This is one of the best private museums in the city and houses an impressive collection, mainly of sacred art and sculptures, consisting of donations by the sculptor Frederic Marès Deulovol from 1940 onwards.

The collection brings together works of art from every corner of Spain that the sculptor visited on his travels, and you can also admire some pieces of Greek and Carthaginian art and several polychrome wooden carvings from the 12th to the 14th centuries.

The Vocation of Saint Peter, a 12th-century work, and the Holy Burial from the 16th century, are some of the valuable works on show.

Leaving the Marès Museum, you find the Lloctinent's (or Lieutenant's) Palace only 30

Coat of arms of the Casa de la Almoina

metres away. Until 1994 this was where the archives of the Crown of Aragon were kept, a privilege that it currently shares with the modern building located next to the Estació del Nord bus station, inaugurated in 1993. The Palace is now used for exhibitions and formal events and the more modern building is equipped for the custody, research and archiving of the works.

Frederic Marès Museum, entrance and interior.

Archive of Aragón   Church of Santa Àgata.   *Plaça del Rei.*

The collections kept in the archive, mainly dating from the Spanish civil war, put the General Archive of the Crown of Aragon on a par with two of the best stocked archives in Spain, the Indias and Simancas Archives.

As further evidence of the sheer number of fascinating places that you find at every step in Barcelona's Gothic Quarter, while you entered the Lloctinent's Palace by the door next to the cathedral, when you leave through the other door you are immediately struck by the sight of the Plaça del Rei. Full of Medieval atmosphere, this square is formed by the Lloctinent's Palace and the Lookout Tower of King Martí, dating from 1555. Here you will find the huge Saló del Tinell council room and the Gothic-style Chapel of Santa Àgata, built in the 14th century. This chapel houses one of the most important paintings in the Catalan Gothic style, the Altarpiece of the Constable (or constables) by Jaume Huguet. It is worth knowing that a visit to these last three monuments is included in a tour offered by the City History Museum, also

located in the square, in the Casa Clariana-Padellàs. This museum includes a subterranean section that takes you right below the square, where you can admire Roman remains and the foundations of the Cathedral from the Visigothic period.

As you make your way out towards nearby Via Laietana you pass by a bronze sculpture of Ramón Berenguer the Great mounted on a charger, work of the sculptor Llimona,

Saló del Tinell.

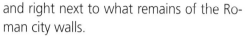
Sculpture of Ramón Berenguer in the square of the same name.

and right next to what remains of the Roman city walls.

The interior courtyard of the Gothic house in nearby Carrer Paradís conceals the remains of what was the Roman Temple of Augustus, of which four large Corinthian columns are still standing.

In Carrer del Bisbe is the Bishop's Palace and the Casa dels Canonges (Canonry). This narrow street facing one of the doors of the Cathedral leads into the famous Plaça de Sant Felip Neri square, where time seems to stand still in the peaceful atmosphere of this secret and beautiful corner of the city.

Carrer del Bisbe leads to the Plaça de Sant Jaume, passing under the pretty Pont de Bisbe bridge. Once in the square, a spectacular space opens out before you, presided over by the buildings that form the political centre of the city, with Barcelona's City Hall (Ajuntament) on one side, and the Palace of the Generalitat (the Catalan Government) on the other.

Plaça Felip Neri.

Façade of the 'Casa dels Canónges'.

Barcelona City Hall in plaça Sant Jaume.

Catalan Government building and details. Construction began in 1403 under the orders of Marc Safont. The original building, set on land acquired by 'La Diputat del General' as the Generalitat or Catalan Government was then known, was extended a century later with the 'Pati dels Tarongers' courtyard and adjoining rooms, with the façade on the Plaça Sant Jaume and the Baroque façades in the north wing being added in the 18th century.

15

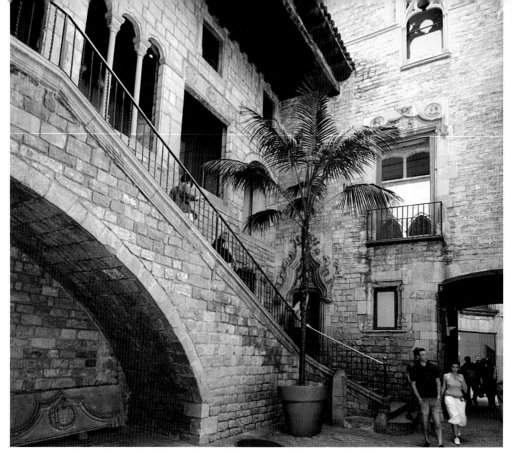

Entrance to the Picasso Museum.

Medieval Barcelona, the Picasso Museum, the Maeght Gallery, and Santa Maria del Mar

No stroll around Medieval Barcelona should start without first hearing about one of the most emblematic and mythical streets of the city, Carrer Montcada. Its walls literally speak, as stone reliefs of the fine old coats of arms that appear along its walls reflect part of the history of ancient Barcino.

This narrow, enchanting street has its origins in the 12th and 13th centuries, when it served to link the old district with the maritime area. However, it was not until the 14th century that its houses were replaced with the construction of the beautiful, sumptuous palaces you see today, making it the centre of the most elegant and stylish district in the whole of the Barcelona of its day.

Framed by this incomparable setting of so much imposing mediaeval architecture is the Picasso Museum, which occupies three

Works by Picasso.

palaces: the Palau de Berenguer d'Aguilar, the Palau del Baró de Castellet, and the Palau Meca, recently also taking in the Mauri and Finestres palaces.

The Picasso Museum first opened to the public on 9 March 1963. With its collection of more than 3,500 works of the Malagan genius, it houses one of the best collections of the artists' work, and is considered to be one of the most important museums in Barcelona. This priceless artistic legacy came about thanks to a generous donation by Jaume Sabartés, personal friend and secretary of Picasso, in the form of the collection of works with which the museum opened. After the death of Sabartés, Picasso himself donated an early portrait of his friend, painted in 1901, and the collection of 58 works on the Meninas series, also promising to go on adding to the museum's collection with future donations. This promise was fulfilled in 1970, with the donation of nearly 1,000 works spanning different styles and techniques. After his death, the painter's widow donated a magnificent collection of more than 40 items of pottery, his heirs gave 117 original engravings, and there were more individual donations and gifts from other galleries. Although a visit to the museum is clearly not to be missed, Carrer Montcada has other less evident charms that make it worthwhile setting aside some time for a peaceful but fascinating stroll. From north to south, you can admire the small Chapel of Marcús, which still retains some reliefs from its Romanesque origins on its walls; the 14th-century Palau del Marqués de Lló, a palace currently in use as the temporary headquarters of the DHUB (Design Hub), and the Palau Nadal, which exhibits an extensive collection of Pre-Columbian Art in what is now the home of the Barbier-Mueller Museum.

Other unmissable visits include the Casa

Small Pre-Columbian statues from the collection of the Barbier-Mueller Museum.

Palau del Marquès de Lió.

Detail of the Palau del Marquès de Lió.

Palau Cervelló, now the Maeght Gallery.

Maeght Gallery.

Cervelló-Giudice, the 15th century building currently occupied by the Maeght Gallery, and the sumptuous 12th-century Palau Dalmases, which houses the Òmnium Cultural association. In fact, the whole of Carrer Montcada acts as a lovely and often surprising showcase of the Mediaeval city.

As if to put the palaces already visited into context and as an impressive climax to your stroll, Carrer Montcada ends with the sight of one of the most significant religious monuments in Barcelona: the Church of Santa Maria del Mar.

The church was first mentioned at the end of the first millennium A.D. Its construction was begun by architect Berenguer de Montagut and completed by Ramón Despuig, in the Catalan Gothic style, distinguishable from European Gothic by the domination of horizontal lines and the predominance of solid panels over empty spaces. Its per-

Santa Maria del Mar. Façade.

fectly finished exterior is a fine example of this style, although the two octagonal side towers belong to different eras. A figure of the Saviour flanked by Our Lady and Saint John crowns the tympanum. The entrance portal has a singular beauty and the whole of the façade itself belongs to the first half of the 14th century, although the upper rose window was destroyed by an earthquake in 1428, being replaced in the 15th century by the present window, in Flamboyant Gothic.

Also known as the Cathedral of the Sea (the title of the best-seller by Ildefonso Falcones), the interior of Santa Maria is presided over by a great central nave and two side naves, separated by slim octagonal columns. The buttresses in the side walls divide the small chapels. Over the crypt a fine presbytery can be seen, dating from the end of the Spanish Civil War, replacing the former structure, destroyed during the war.

Declared a Historical and Artistic Monument of National Interest in 1931, its fine acoustics also make this religious buildings one of the best of its kind for concerts, which are held here all year round.

Rose window.

Interior of the Basilica. >

Plaça de Catalunya, general view.

Aerial view of the Rambla.

A stroll along the Rambla

Plaça de Catalunya, considered the nerve centre of the city, is the starting point of a world-famous stroll, down the La Rambla of Barcelona. Formerly the watercourse serving the city, the Rambla (or Les Rambles, the plural form) it ran along the outside of the ancient city walls of Barcino, built in the 13th century. With the passage of time, the walls came to restrict the city's spectacular growth, and most of them were demolished. The old river-bed was then covered over to create the Rambla that we see today, one of the most original and emblematic avenues of the city, an absolute must for any tourists arriving in Barcelona.

Canaletas Fountain.

The first attraction the Rambla has to offer is the Fountain of Canaletas, made out of forged iron in the 19th century. This spectacular four-spouted fountain crowned by a lamp-post with four lamps has its own special popular legend, that any traveller drinking from any of its four spouts is bound to come back to the city.

From here down, the different stretches of this popular Barcelona street (each of the 5 'Rambles" with its own special name) will fascinate you with the diversity of their architecture, culture and art on this unique itinerary. At the fountain, you are just a hundred metres away from the impressive

The Rambla in Barcelona. The city's residents are convinced that the contrasting colours, ambiences, scents, activities and idiosyncracies of this street in the Catalan capital make it unique.

Church of Belén - altarpiece.

building that once housed the Royal Academy of the Arts and Sciences and since 1929 has been the Poliorama Theatre. On the same side, at the junction with Carrer Pintor Fortuny, the building that once belonged to the Philippines Tobacco Company has been converted into a modern hotel, practically next door to the Church of Belén, one of the few examples of Baroque architecture surviving in Barcelona, and the old Jesuit Convent. Its construction started in 1681, although the works did not finish until 1732. This is a church with a single nave and numerous side chapels, whose striking original decoration was destroyed in a fire at the start of the Spanish Civil War. During the Christmas period, the Church of Belén offers one of the most-visited display of nativity scenes in the city. Opposite the church, on the junction with Carrer Portaferrisa, is the Palau Mojà, which once had the privilege of accommodating the famous poet Hyacinth Verdaguer, a protégé of the Comillas family who acquired the palace from the Mojà family that gave it its name.

An unusual tiled fountain with a frieze of the city walls can be found at the other side of the junction with Carrer Portaferrisa.

Next, turn right along Carrer del Carmen to reach the buildings that formed the former Hospital de Santa Creu, begun in the 15th century although not completed until the 18th century. Nowadays it houses the Library of Catalonia, the Institute of Catalan Studies and the Academy of Medicine

Fountain at the entry to Carrer Portaferrisa.

Hospital de la Santa Creu.

in the former House of Convalescence. A lovely garden takes you down towards Carrer Hospital where you pass the classrooms of the Massana School, attended by many of the city's future artists.

Retracing you steps you find the Plaça dels Àngels and the Barcelona Contemporary Art Museum (MACBA), a spectacular white serene modern building designed by architect Richard Meier, which opened its doors to the public in 1995. The appearance of the surrounding district certainly provides a striking contrast to this modern and complex building, giving the whole area a unique character.

MACBA houses works from the MACBA Foundation collection, which is constantly growing thanks to contributions from the

Modern building containing the Barcelona Museum of Contemporary Art (MACBA)

private sector. For one reason or another, a visit to this museum has become a must for everyone with an interest in art and culture. Every part of the Rambla has its own unique personality. On the Rambla de les Flors with its flower stalls, you can pay a visit to the Palau de la Virreina, built as the home of the widow of a former Viceroy of Peru, from whom it takes its name), admiring the building's Baroque style and its majestic Rococo decoration. One of the most important and perfect examples of 18th-century Catalan civil architecture, it is currently used for exhibitions of art and culture linked to events in the city.

In 1941, it was declared a Historical and Artistic Monument of National Interest.

Moving on down, you cannot miss the Boquería Market.

Some say that the best way to get to know a city is by visiting its markets. If this is true, it would be unforgivable not to pay a highly worth-while visit to one of the most typical and best-stocked municipal food markets in the city: the Boquería, also known as the Market of Sant Josep.

Palau de la Virreina.

More than 300 colourful stalls vie with each other in the range of products they offer, and you would be unlucky not to come across those special foodstuffs that are so hard to find in any other market. Meat, tropical fruit, fish, root and green vegetables, game birds: whatever you fancy for the kitchen, you will certainly find in this market. While you look around, take some time to admire the architecture of this spectacular building, which still has its original 18th-century transparent iron and glass roof.

Boquería Market. Fascinating mix of colours, smells, tastes and people of every nationality.

Pía de l'Os. Mosaic by Miró.

The Pla de l'Os (or Pla de la Boquería) is a space on the street outside the market where the famous painter, Joan Miró, created his own particular homage to the Boquería: this splendid mosaic painted on the ground could may be the only work of art that you can actually walk over on a daily basis without the risk of being told off! Certainly an original way of interpreting art.

Before continuing your 'vertical' itinerary down the Rambla, turn off left into Carrer Cardenal Casañas to visit the Church of Santa Maria del Pi (Blessed Mary of the Pine Tree) in the square of the same name, built in the Catalan Gothic style and founded in 1332. It has an austere single nave and side chapels. Two of the most interesting of these are the chapels of San Miguel and Our Lady of the Forsaken, both dating from the 18th century. The stained glass windows in the side doors are creations of Antoni Viladomat.

The main façade gives onto the Plaça del Pi - its most outstanding features are the arabesques of the arches of the main porch and the majestic upper rose window with twelve arms, considered by many to be the biggest in the world. An octagonal bell tower 54 metres high adds to the interest of this magnificent church. The square beside it, Sant Josep Oriol, is a favourite with

Church of Santa Maria del Pi and baptismal font.

Relaxing over a coffee and art street market in Plaça Sant Josep Oriol.

artists displaying their works to the public at weekends, and the Plaça del Pi square next door often has fairs where family businesses set out stalls full of tasty produce and local wares.

Back on the Rambla, the Gran Teatre del Liceu (Liceu Opera House) is one of the prides of Barcelona. The original building, the work of architect Miquel Garriga i Roca, was inaugurated on 4 April 1847 on the site formerly occupied by an old Convent of the Barefoot Trinitarians, and accommodated approximately 3,500 people, only surpassed by the La Scala opera house in Milan. Over the years, the theatre has survived several disasters. The first of these was the fire in 1861, after which it had to be refurbished first by the architect Josep Oriol Mestres, and later remodelled by Pere Falqués, who had taken part in the original construction. Later, in 1893, two bombs were thrown into the stalls by an anarchist, only one of which exploded, but still causing more than twenty deaths among the audience.

Finally, there was the terrible fire of 1994 which completely destroyed the theatre, leaving only the main façade standing. After a great deal of work and detailed studies that permitted its rebuilding and extension, the 'Liceu' was re-inaugurated at the end of 1999.

Façade of the Gran Teatre del Liceu.

Resuming our tour, we soon arrive at the Plaça Reial, one of the most lively and long-lived squares in Barcelona. Located on the site of a former Capuchin convent, the Plaça Reial has a rectangular layout with uniform houses set above fine ground-floor arches that echo the cloisters of the former church. A spectacular central foun-

Majestic image showing the interior of the opera theatre and details.

A stroll around the Plaça Reial, located just beside the Rambla, is a must for every visitor.

tain attracts a multicultural collection of street artists and musicians, and under the shade of the arches, the square's traditional restaurants and beer houses offer cooling drinks and tasty local dishes.

There is even some of the work of brilliant Barcelona architect Gaudí, in the form of the lamp-posts that still help light up the square.

Further down still, turn right into Carrer Nou de La Rambla, which runs between the Rambla and El Parallel. Only 50 metres down the street you can visit one of the architectural jewels left by Antoni Gaudí to Barcelona, the Güell Palace. Its remarkable façade has parabolic arches, with ornamental ironwork built into the wall itself. Particularly well known features are its chimneys, adorned with mosaics in bright colours. This monument was declared an Historical and Artistic Monument of National Interest in 1969, and was included in UNESCO's World Heritage List in 1984. Returning to the Rambla, you are nearing the end of your walk. The Plaça del Teatre offers the sight of artists of all ages and origins displaying their talent. You can find or sit for caricatures and paintings in every style and using the most imaginative approaches.

The square has a monument to 'Pitarra', the pseudonym of the founder of modern

The Palau Güell will provide inspiration to keen photographers.

 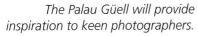   

The Rambla.

< *Teatre Principal.*

Catalan theatre and is overlooked by the venerable façade of the first city's first theatre, the Teatre Principal.

The Santa Monica Art Centre on the right occupies the space of the former convent of same name, which fell into ruin in the 19th century. Now restored, it hosts a series of cultural and artistic exhibitions.

Opposite the Art Centre, an intriguing little narrow street opens out, leading down to a tiny square. This belongs to the Barcelona Wax Museum, with more than 300 figures

< *Monument to 'Pitarra'.*

Sta. Mónica Art Centre.

representing different personalities portrayed in environments representing their era. The museum was founded by filmmaker Enrique Alarcón.

They are so many attractions on the Rambla of Barcelona that we have taken for granted some of the aspects and personalities that give it its special, entertaining atmosphere that make it so difficult to compare with anywhere else: the flower stalls, newsagents, traditional shops, terraces, stall-holders, artists, human statues, tarotcard readers, poets, musicians and so many others who form part of this incomparable and unforgettable environment.

Main façade of the Barcelona Wax Museum, ticket office and details of its interior.

The Drassanes Reials, a building that currently hosts Barcelona's Maritime Museum.

Sant Pau del Camp church, the Columbus Monument and the La Ribera district

We have already remarked how one of the most memorable periods in the history of Barcelona was its Medieval era, when the city's power around the Mediterranean rivalled that of Genoa and Venice. At that time, city life focused on the sea, and the building of great galleons and warships was a flourishing activity, particularly during the 14th and 15th centuries.

The Barcelona Maritime Museum now occupies three large sections of the 'Drassanes' (shipyards) of the time, using them to display some spectacular ships which are witnesses to the city's maritime heyday. There is normally an interesting temporary exhibition as well. The sheer size and perfect state of conservation of the building ensures that these ancient shipyards are admired and their importance recognised throughout the world. Next to the museum you can see a small section of what remains of the city walls of the former Barcino, the result of the latest reconstruction in 1939. In 1976, the site was declared a Historical and Artistic Monument of National Interest.

Not so long ago, the street known as Paral. lel was Barcelona's favourite entertainment district. But one by one, theatres like El Molino, the Arnau, the Victoria and many others have been disappearing, although so far not completely, from this scene

In its day, Paral.lel was the centre of the world of entertainment in Barcelona.

Monument to Raquel Meller, in the Avinguda del Paral.lel.

(there are plans to restore some of them to their original use). Also on the bright side, there has been an increase in the number of hotels and restaurants here, due to the growth in office space and the proximity of the Trade Fair precinct. The Monument to artiste Raquel Meller survives alongside the Arnau, and some posters still keep alive memories of another era.

Not far from the theatres and the Maritime Museum, along Carrer Sant Pau, stands a small but charming church, the Church of Sant Pau del Camp (Saint Paul of the countryside), on the site of a former Benedictine abbey. This 11th-century Catalan-Romanesque church preserves remains that pre-date this era, among them the gravestone of Wifred II, dated 912. Recently tours of the church have been started, and visitors can admire its single cloister with trefoil arches, its façade featuring Lombard arches and inlays of stone figures. A twin-windowed bell tower without bells crowns the building. Although somewhat off the beaten track and small in size, this lovely church is well worth a visit. It was one of the first monuments to be given the title of Monument of National Interest, back in 1879.

At some points of your tour you have been near the sea, but your next stop will give you the chance to stop and contemplate the waters of the port at your leisure. Continue down to the very end of the Rambla to Portal de Pau square to see one of the best-known symbols of the city, the Monu-

Main façade and interiors of the Church of Sant Pau del Camp, which has been described as 'a Romanesque jewel in a Gothic city'.

ment to Christopher Columbus (Cristobal Colon in Catalan), built for the inauguration of the first Universal Exposition held in Barcelona in 1888. The monument commemorates the visit made by Admiral Columbus to the city, to show off to the Spanish Kings his finds on his voyage of discovery. It may have a slender silhouette, but you will have no trouble getting to the top of the 87 metre-high monument thanks to a small visitors' lift. From the top you can enjoy one of the best views over the port, the World Trade Centre, the modern Hotel Vela, the Ramblas and right across the city of Barcelona. At its foot you can browse for curiosities in a small collectibles market held

The monument to Columbus in Barcelona rises 87 metres above sea level with the statue of Christopher Columbus set on high, gazing out towards the Americas.

Details of the base of the monument.

Hotel Vela in the foreground and general view of the beach.

sportsmen and women and teams, to offer up their triumphs to the Patron Saint.

Continue to where the road crosses Via Laietana and you will see the imposing Post Office building, a Monumental construction dating from the early 20th century. Two magnificent towers stand at either end of the main façade, the tower on the Via Laietana side being higher, and the building itself has three floors.

Basilica of La Mercè.

every weekend. The monument is due to be refurbished in the near future.

With your back to the sea, turn right now along the Passeig de Colón, a narrow street running alongside the Military Government Headquarters, and you will come to the Plaça de la Mercè, the square of the Basilica de la Mercè, dedicated to the patron saint of the city. The image of Our Lady is a beautiful Gothic statue carved by Pere Moragues in 1361. This former Mercedarian convent has a single nave, side chapels, and Late Baroque cladding in marble and stucco. An un-written but still observed custom is a visit to the church by the city's

Taking a short detour back uphill, this time up Via Laietana, you can turn off to visit the Santa Caterina market on your right along Avinguda de Francesc Cambó, a particular attraction being its famous and controversial curved, multi-coloured roof, designed by architects Enric Miralles and Benedetta Tagliabue. You can also eat well here. Descending again seawards and turning

Market of Santa Caterina.

Post Office building.

Arches of the Pla del Palau.

Fisherman's dock.

left at the Post Office along the Passeig d'Isabel II, near the Pla de Palau, you will find the Porxos d'en Xifré. This is a block of houses with a beautiful arcade of 21 arches, where the Set Portes restaurant is justly famous for the quality of its paellas. Take any street down towards the sea and you will find yourself in Barceloneta, one of the city's most authentic and characterful districts. Once a breeding ground of expert sailors and fishermen, it still preserves the

colourful atmosphere of the neighbour-
hood of the 'tascas marineras' (sea-farers'
taverns) and has a well-maintained beach.
Old sea-wolves continue to brave the waters in search of fish to sell at the Moll de
Pescadors and Rellotge docks, where you
can still observe the traditional sales at the
fish market.

Possibly after stopping off for a delicious
seafood meal in any of the excellent Barceloneta restaurants, retrace your steps

Beaches of Barceloneta.

Ciutadela Park.

Pond in Ciutadela Park.

to Avinguda Marquès de l'Argentera you come to the Parc de la Ciutadella (or Citadel). This is the second-largest green area in the city and consists of a patchwork of pretty avenues set around landscaped gardens and grass. Construction of the park began in 1871 as a special attraction for the Universal Exposition of 1888. The land now given over to the park was originally cleared by demolition of part of the Ribera District after the War of the Spanish Succession in the 18th century, to build the Citadel which formed part of the military strategy of the day by King Felipe V to subjugate the city.

The centre of the park, the former parade ground, is now graced by an oval pond in which stands the statue 'Despair', one of the most admired works of the Catalan sculptor, Llimona. Opposite the pond is the building of the Catalan Parliament.

A small lake with boats and a short stroll separate this part of the park from the huge monumental fountain with waterfall, a French-inspired architectural group designed by Catalan architect Fontseré, with the collaboration of Antoni Gaudí.

Another fascinating and enigmatic figure is the statue of the Lady with the Umbrella in the grounds of the Dolphinarium, a show

Zoology Museum.

Lady with Umbrella.

with friendly dolphins which will delight both the youngest members of the family and grown-ups alike.

The Geology and Zoology Museums are both inside the park, just a hundred metres apart. The latter is housed in a Modernista building designed by Catalan architect Domènech i Montaner and was mainly used as a restaurant during the Exposition. But the park has many other spots and spaces where you can find entertainment or space for contemplation: the Hivernacle, by Josep Amargós, and the Umbracle, by Fontseré, are good examples.

A considerable area of Ciutadela Park is

taken up by Barcelona Zoo. Considered one of the best in Europe, it was inaugurated in 1894 and since then has introduced ongoing improvements to its habitats in a series of refurbishments to enhance the comfort of its 'inhabitants'. For decades, the zoo's name was intimately linked to it's most famous resident, the albino gorilla known as 'Floquet de Neu' (Snowflake or 'Copito de nieve' in Spanish), the first and only example of its kind ever found, creating great excitement throughout his life until he died in 2003.

In the area of the park furthest from the sea is a great central throughway, the Pas-

Details of the Zoo.

seig de Lluís Companys, ending in the Arc de Triomf (Triumphal Arch), also built for the 1888 Exposition. In the reddish stone used for its construction you can see scenes representing the power of the industry and trade of the era. The monument is crowned by a royal coat of arms, with the shield of Barcelona lower down, linked with the emblems of the other Spanish provinces.

Not far from the park is the Estació de França train station, the result of the extension of the original building put up on the site in 1930. The present station is an enormous structure of metal arches more

Arc de Triomf.

than 30 metres high, with a spectacular vestibule designed by Raimon Durán and Salvador Soteras. But increasing passenger numbers caused Sants Railway Terminal to take on much of the traffic, letting this veteran station recover some of the tranquillity of former times.

Opposite the main entrance and only 100 metres away is the old market of the El Born District, in recent years the subject of some controversy, since improvement works unexpectedly uncovered Roman remains from the ancient city of Barcino and caused a conflict of interest between conservation and present use, eventually solved by a combination of the two concepts.

< *França Station.*

Borne Market.

Route of Modernisme: Rambla de Catalunya, Passeig de Gràcia, Diagonal

The Plaça de Catalunya is where most things start in the city. Returning to the top of the Rambla and crossing the square you will enter the Rambla de Catalunya, the continuation up towards Tibidabo mountain of the Rambla itself. This boulevard is lined with glamorous shops and numerous terraces where you can spend the day shopping or simply relax over your favourite drink.

At its junction with Gran Vía, a refreshing centrepiece in the form of a fountain and

Flirtatious Giraffe and Meditating Bull by Josep Granyer mark the beginning and the end of the Rambla de Catalunya

Building of the Antoni Tapies Foundation.

some fine Modernista buildings will attract your attention (Modernisme is a Catalan fin de siècle art movement). This is a long street but you can take your time browsing in the shops, or threading your way up between the tables on its terraces. When you reach the intersection with Carrer Aragon, on your right you will see the fine building that houses the foundation of world famous artist Antoni Tàpies, once used by the publishing firm, Montaner i Simó. The Foundation was created in 1984 by Tàpies to encourage the study of modern art and to provide a showcase for his extensive work. The adaptation of the building is unusual for its curious solution to the problem of its difference in height with adjacent buildings, by topping the façade with a metallic structure that supports a tangle of wire. This was controversial in its day but over time has become sign of identity. The wire sculpture has assumed its own personality, and has been baptised 'Cloud and Chair' due to its curious shape.

Casa Serra.

You will see other striking buildings all the way up this street, but the most outstanding of all is right at the top, near the junction with Avinguda Diagonal. This is the Casa Serra, currently headquarters of Barcelona Provincial Council, a building in Modernista style designed by Catalan architect Josep Puig i Cadafalch. This notable early nineteenth-century construction was originally designed as a family mansion and once included a fine garden. The current building is a mix of styles - Renaissance, Mudejar, Gothic and Plateresque.

At this point, you are now approaching the most emblematic street in the city, the Passeig de Gràcia. Lined with designer stores stocked with haute couture, this is also the setting for the most striking Modernista buildings in Barcelona.

In fact, so rich is the mixture of architectural styles seen on its façades that part of the street is known as the 'Manzana de la Discordia' ('Block of Discord', in Spanish), in an allusion to the obvious dizzy contrasts. Cutting across Carrer Corsega where there

'Block of Discord'.

La Pedrera.

are some pleasant cafes, you reach the top of the Passeig, at its junction with Diagonal. The first building you pass as you head down the street on the right is the Palau Robert, headquarters of the Tourist Board which also hosts temporary exhibitions. Continuing downwards, you will see on the other side of the street the emblematic designer shop Vicenç. Once owned by painter Ramón Casas and designed by Ro-

Palau Robert.

vira i Rabassa it is now full of the latest in interior design and opens up some of the building as display space.

Still on the same side, continuing down to the junction with Carrer Provença you find one of the high points of the architecture of Antoni Gaudí. This is 'La Pedrera' (literally 'the Quarry'), so-called due to its unique external appearance, crafted in stone and iron brought from Vilafranca del Penedés. Built between 1906 and 1910, the originality of the architecture is enhanced by its undulating shape, giving the building a curious feeling of mobility.

The interior is a challenge to traditional aesthetics. As soon as you enter the building you come across highly original shapes and drawings that entirely cover structural elements like columns and ceiling. But the most surprising aspect is the absence of a grand stairway for its residents, who have to get to their flats by lift or by climbing the service stairway. These stairs, and the doors

La Pedrera.
Some details.

and designs of the windows that you observe as you climb upwards reveal the genius of the architect from Reus. Still further evidence of Gaudí's originality is found in the figures on the roof terrace, so startling that it is impossible to imagine any mind other than that of Gaudí inventing them at the time. Ventilation turrets clad in fragments of different-coloured broken bottles, wildly-twisting chimneys and figures with crazy profiles are some of the motifs that caused the building to be nominated as a Histori-

cal Artistic Monument of National Interest in 1969 and later, in 1984, recognised by UNESCO as a World Heritage building. Since 1999, visits to La Pedrera have become even more interesting with the opening of one of the apartments, decorated in the style of the era when it was built. It is also the venue for prestigious temporary art exhibitions, with free entry.

As you leave, stunned by the beauty of this unique house, you may think it impossible to find another architectural jewel even half as impressive. You would be wrong, because only three blocks away on the other side of the Passeig is the second master work of Gaudí, the Casa Batlló, at number 43, on the corner with Carrer Aragón. The original building was totally reworked by the famous architect at the request of textile impresario, Josep Batlló, to produce the outstanding work you can see today.

After La Pedrera and the discrete beiges of its exterior, the façade of this building will come as a shock. Its striking colouring is the result of combining pottery and glass to create some remarkable tonal effects. Equally impressive is the shape of its balconies, designed in wrought-iron to resemble a series of carnival masks. The roof that rises above this remarkable frontage incorporates a series of super-imposed tiles, for all the world like the multi-coloured scales of a beautiful fish, and an unusual turret topped with a cross.

The steep slope of the roof is broken by a dormer window crowned by a circular tow-

Casa Batlló. Its windows fit perfectly into the architecture.

er, where the inscription: 'Jesus, Mary and Joseph' is picked out in gold letters, and there is a four-armed cross. As with La Pedrera, the figures on the roof of the Casa Batlló are spectacular, with their slender lines and striking colouration. As you can imagine, the Casa Batlló has also been declared a World Heritage building, in 2005

Next door to the Casa Batlló is the Casa Amatller, built by the architect Puig i Cadafalch in 1898. Totally different from its neighbour, this monumental building is characterised by a Neo Gothic façade, inundated with colour and crowned by a roof edged with a peculiar step pattern. Inside the vestibule are some reliefs depicting allegories portraying the fine arts, and a Saint George confronting a dragon. In 1976, it was declared a Historical and Artistic Monument of National Interest. At the end of the same block at No. 43 (junction with Consell de Cent) is the Casa Lleó Morera, designed Domènech i Montaner and dating from 1905. Its external façade is covered with beautiful details and sculptural pieces and it is topped by a shrine restored by Óscar Tusquets and Carles Díaz following the original, which was badly damaged during the Spanish Civil War. The whole building is a perfect expression of Modernista floral decoration. The interior of the vestibule is a homage to the taste of the Catalan bourgeoisie of the era when it was built.

Doubling back one block to Carrer Valencia and crossing the road again, is yet another particularly interesting building, at the junction of Passeig de Gràcia (No. 66) and Car-

Casa Amatller.

rer Valencia opposite the Hotel Majestic: the Casa Marfà, with its ornate Modernista exterior and interior.

Continue back up Passeig de Gràcia passing the Pedrera again to the junction with Diagonal, and going one block down Diagonal to the junction with Pau Claris, you will find another fine Modernista building, the Casa Comalat, at number 442, the back of which faces onto Carrer Corsega. Further down at number 416-420 is the house known as the 'Casa de les Punxes' (literally 'house of spikes'), a whole block with irregular shaped pointed gables that takes its name from the sharp forms of its showy towers. This is another legacy left to Barcelona by architect Josep Puig i Cadafalch, who was responsible for building it between 1903 and 1905. Except for the lower storey, clad in stone,

Casa Lleó Morera.

Casa Quadras.

Casa Comalat.

63

Casa de 'Les Punxes' and details of the façade.

the rest of the façade is of reddish brick, adorned with details in coloured ceramic work and wrought-iron. The work mixes the Gothic and Spanish Plateresque styles.

At number 373 Diagonal is the Casa Quadras, a small mansion dating from 1904 built on the site of an old rented house reformed by the Baron de Quadras. The house has many Gothic details in its interior and a magnificent façade that bears some resemblance to the magnificent palaces in the Gothic Quarter. Once the Museum of Music, it is now the home of Barcelona's Casa Asia, with an extensive programme of events.

Palau de la Musica Catalana and some splendid details.

The Palau de la Musica Catalana

This breathtakingly beautiful Modernista building, representing the high point of the career of architect Domènech i Montaner, was built between 1905 and 1908. The Palau de la Musica Catalana was designed as the venue for concerts by the Or-

feó Català, a choral group founded in the late 19th century by Lluís Millet and Amadeu Vives, great patrons of Catalan music. One mystery is how this magnificent building was ever erected in an environment of such small narrow streets, giving it almost a domestic feel. One of the most representative views of the concert hall can be seen by standing at the corner of the building and looking upwards to the first floor. From this point you can see the sculpture by Miquel Blay representing Saint George in his armour in battle position, surrounded by a group of everyday characters and a beautiful maiden who symbolises music. This work is considered to be one of the masterpieces of realistic Catalan sculpture. As with Gaudí's buildings, the lower part of the façade is ornamented with inlays of small pieces of ceramic in a vivid range

Impressive multicoloured ceiling light.

Grandeur of the concert hall and details of the stage.

of colours and varied shapes, a technique known as 'Trencadis'. Once inside, you can see an oval auditorium that holds 2,000 people. The columns, marble floors, huge polychrome windows, enormous stairway, abundant ceramic decoration, impressive

Palau de la Musica.

the work of Lluís Bru, and flanked by a set of musical muses in ceramic, also by Bru and Eusebi Arnau.

A magnificent stained glass sky-light designed in the form of an inverted dome provides the main lighting in the concert hall and is just one of its remarkable decorative elements. In 1909 the Palau de la Musica Catalana was awarded the Prize for Best Building of the Year by Barcelona City Council, and in 1997, UNESCO declared it a World Heritage building.

organ and host of other decorative elements, give the place a quality that is impossible to compare with anything else you will have seen. It is presided over by an organ bearing the coat of arms of Catalonia,

Ticket office and mosaics.

Upper Barcelona: Pedralbes and Tibidabo

Take metro line 3 to Palau Reial. In 1921, Eusebi Bona i Puig and Francesc de Paula Nebot began work on building the Palau de Pedralbes, built on land ceded by the Güell family, which was to become the palatial residence of King Alfons XIII. However, history sometimes takes unexpected turns, and the architects' intentions were frustrated: the palace was used to house various personalities during the Second Republic, and subsequently the dictator, General Franco, stayed there on his visits to the city. From 1960 on, the palace threw its doors open to the public, converted into the Museum of Ceramics (it now houses part of the DHUB Costume and Textiles museum as well). The Ceramics Museum is considered to be among the best of its kind in Spain, with works in its collection that date back to the 13th century. Al-

Plaza de Francesc Macià.

Palau de Pedralbes.

though the palace has now lost most of its most unusual fittings, you can still find some beautiful furniture and table lamps to admire.

Near the palace, in Avinguda de Pedralbes, you should take the opportunity to visit

Dragon.

Güell pavilions.

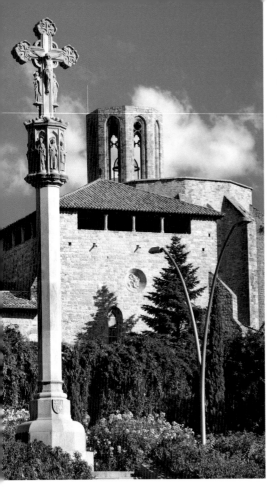

the Pavilions of the Güell Estate, another of the creations of Antoni Gaudí within the Barcelona city limits. Although possibly not the best-known of the artist's works, the main gate has magnificent wrought iron ornamentation of undeniable originality and appeal, particularly the menacing figure of the dragon.

Continuing up Avinguda de Pedralbes, Pedralbes Monastery and Museum is an enchanting corner, a haven of peace in the bustle of the great city.

Elisenda de Montcada, the last wife of King Jaume II, knew that her husband wanted to be buried next to his first wife, so she decided to build this monastery as the last abode of the monarch. Construction of the monastery began in 1326 under the supervision of the Order of the Poor Clares. One of the main elements of this monument is its famous three-floored cloister, considered by many to be among the finest of its kind in the world in the ogival style. The church's interior consists of a single nave, with a series of side chapels mainly used for the tombs of important personalities, among them Elisenda de Montcada herself. For some years now, rooms in the monastery have housed a magnificent museum of works of art and furniture, mainly from the 14th century. The building was declared a Historical and Artistic Monument of National Interest in 1991.

Returning to Diagonal to near where the motorway crosses the city boundary to Esplugues is the Ciutat Esportiva (sport city)

Monastery of Pedralbes.

F.C. Barcelona football stadium.

of FC Barcelona football club. Tourists or visitors arriving in Barcelona may not think this is a cultural monument, but there are few Catalans who are not convinced of the importance and influence of the club in Catalan society.

You should now make your way to Plaça John Kennedy (possibly via returning to Plaça de Catalunya to catch the Ferrocarils de la Generalitat railway), where you will find one of the most traditional and popular ways of visiting Tibidabo Mountain: an enchanting old tramway that ends its run at the funicular railway, which completes your ascent. The popular Catalan name for the old tramway is the 'Tramvia Blau' (blue tramway).

If you have plenty of time, you can devote some of it to visiting the Science Museum, CosmoCaixa, located on the tram route near the Ronda de Dalt ring road.

The Tibidabo Funicular Railway was inaugurated in the early years of the 20th cen-

Tramvia Blau.

Science Museum.

tury and has a run of over 1,150 metres on a single track up the steep slope.

Your unhurried ascent ends in the Amusement Park at Tibidabo, next to the church known as the Expiatory Temple of the Sacred Heart of Jesus, a monument in Neo Gothic style whose building began in 1902 although it was not completed until almost sixty years later after an interminable series of stoppages. The church is crowned by a huge Christ figure that seems to extend its blessing over the entire city, although the nearest site and so the first to receive its blessings is the children's amusement park located almost at the door of the church itself.

Since the Olympic Games in 1992, the profile of the mountain has included the Collserola Communications Tower, an imposing work by the famous architect Norman Foster, created to handle the communications of this important sporting event.

Submarine that points the way (approximately) to the Science Museum.

Tibidabo, an aerial view with the communications tower to the left, the Expiatory Temple of the Sacred Heart and the funfair.

Aerial view of the entire site of Park Güell.

Park Güell and the Sagrada Família: gifts of Gaudí

Some aspects of Park Güell. The combination of stone with nature shows us the Modernista genius of Antonio Gaudí in all its glory.

On the mountainous area of El Carmel and 150 metres above sea level is Park Güell, one of the major and most astonishing works of the architect, created at the initiative of its sponsor, Eusebi Güell. Gaudí was assigned a project which was originally intended to become an English-style resi-

dential estate, containing 60 luxury family dwellings. The idea of the complex failed, and finally only two of the planned houses were built, one being used by Gaudí as his home, although he later moved out to live in the Sagrada Família. Park Güell's outstanding virtue is that it mixes architecture

with nature in a delightful and imaginative way. One of its most characteristic elements is the double stairway at the main entrance to the site, set between the two buildings that stand above the wall of the park. In the centre of the double stairway is the famous multi-coloured dragon, covered in small fragments of mosaic, and there are other equally attractive figures, which Gaudí ornamented using different water effects. The Hall of the Hundred Columns at the top of the stairway was meant to serve as the main market of the complex.

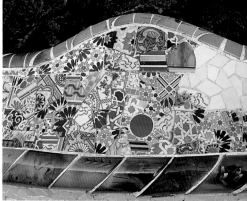

The columns, built in the Doric style and slightly sloping, support a great circular Plaça surrounded by a long, undulating bench clad in small pieces of brightly-coloured mosaic (known as Trencadis). Running between the Hall of the Hundred Columns and the Circular Plaça, an eccentric but attractive and original gallery gives a romantic touch to the park.

The most outstanding construction is the house that was Gaudí's residence between 1906 and 1925, now converted into his House Museum, and in which you can admire part of the furniture designed by the artist and some personal memorabilia. The whole park was declared a World Heritage site by UNESCO in 1984.

After the luxury of a tour of Parc Güell, you can finish off the day by going back down into the city to seek out the Barcelona monument that has possibly become the city's major attraction, and has certainly

sealed Gaudí's reputation as a genius in every part of the world: the Basilica of the Sagrada Família.

This spectacular monument, possibly the most visited in the city, was begun by Gaudí in 1883, inspired by an earlier project of Francesc de Paula Villar under the auspices of the Spiritual Association of Devotees of Saint Joseph and its founder, Josep Maria Bocabella.

The Catalan architect wished to make this church the great modern cathedral of the city. To do this, he designed the complex system of Christian symbolism represented in the church. The initial project consisted of five naves with transept and apse and an external ambulatory, as well as 18 great parabolic spires to symbolise the 12 apostles, the 4 evangelists, Our Lady, and Jesus Christ which rose above the others. One curious fact is that the slightly convex spires and the spiral staircase have inscriptions that are repeated vertically and horizontally. The ends of the pinnacles are clad in a glazed polychrome mosaic and crowned by an impressive cross.

After Gaudí's tragic death, run over by a tram in 1926, the unfinished construction, always under works, was continued following the plans of the original project, and it was only in 1987 that sculptor Josep

The Sagrada Família and details. The masterpiece of Antoni Gaudí.

The Sagrada Família night view and details.

Maria Subirachs created the images for the Passion Façade.

However, the construction of a great work like the Sagrada Família can never be exempt from controversy. Some authorities favoured leaving the work unfinished in the personal form designed by Gaudí, but other equally authorised voices called for it to be continued, arguing that the church had to be finished. Fortunately this second decision prevailed, and so you can now admire the monument in the advanced stage that you see it in today.

To get a better idea of the work, you may like to visit the Museum of the Sagrada Família, located under the four spires of the Passion Façade, where the models and plans for the project's construction are kept.

Montjuïc and the Olympic Ring

You can reach Montjuïc mountain in many ways from several different directions, including walking, bus or funicular. Perhaps the most interesting way for visitors is starting from the metro station of Paral.lel. From there you can take a ride on the Funicular Railway, neglected for years but after its reform for the Olympic Games in 1992 its installations now meet today's standards.

Montjuïc is one of the two hills that surround Barcelona, the other being Tibidabo. On this mountain you can find many amenities of interest to tourists, most dating from the days of the World Fair in 1929, which started off the urbanisation of the site, and from the 1992 Olympic Games.

Left over from the first event on the lower slopes were the Palau Nacional, now the MNAC modern art gallery, the Poble Espanyol (Spanish village) complex, the Magic Fountain (with son et lumière presentations) and the Mies van der Rohe Pavilion,

Aerial view of Montjuïc Olympic exhibition.

Montjuïc Castle and helmet of Jaume I.

a construction referred to by experts as the 'paradigm of modern architecture', and the 1992 Olympics contributed the series of buildings in what is called the Olympic Ring. All over Montjuïc you can enjoy visiting museums, galleries, monuments and green areas, including the Costa i Llobera and Mosén Cinto Verdaguer Gardens, and the Botanical Gardens. The latter specialise in the flora of the five regions in the world with a Mediterranean climate.

Starting at the top, Montjuïc Castle is one of the most impressive constructions on the mountain. This 18th-century fortress was constructed over another castle, built in only thirty days during the 'War of the Segadors', (or reapers) in 1640. Until recently, you could find a Military Museum

Poble Espanyol.

Miró Foundation.

inside the castle grounds with an important collection of arms, armour and vestments of different eras but this was closed in 2009, with some items staying and others to be displayed elsewhere.

From the castle grounds and also from the so-called 'Mayor's Lookout' nearby, as indeed from any point on the mountain, you can enjoy some of the best views over Barcelona and the port.

On your way down the mountain, try to visit the Miró Foundation, a Rationalist construction with one single floor designed in the 1970s by architect Josep Lluís Sert, a friend of the artist. The building is laid out around an inner courtyard, and its exhibition rooms are illuminated by skylights. The Foundation, created by Joan Miró in 1971, was founded to promote the study and dissemination of the painter's works, although it also puts on prestigious temporary exhibitions of contemporary art.

Continuing down Avinguda del Estadi, you soon arrive at the Anell Olímpic or Olympic Ring, a series of installations rehabilitated for the 1992 Olympic Games. They are all magnificent, but particularly impressive is the Lluís Companys Olympic Stadium, built for the World Fair in 1929 and which had already hosted the 2nd Mediterranean Games held in Barcelona in 1955. The stadium, suitably renovated and modernised after suffering years of neglect, was the scenario chosen for the inauguration of the 1992 Olympic Games. The extent of the works meant that only the old façade of the building, a beautiful example of Neo-Classical style, could be preserved. Another of the star constructions of the Games is the Palau Sant Jordi, with a capacity for 17,000 spectators and often used for concerts. It was designed by Japanese architect Arata Isozaki, who applied the most advanced technologies to this sporting venue, particularly in the spectacular structure of its roof.

The slim Calatrava Tower, situated between the Palau Reial building and the Bernat Picornell Swimming Pools, marks the high point of the sporting heritage left behind in the city by the 1992 Olympic Games.

Diverting your attention for a moment, if you headed up the mountain past the Olympic Ring from the Caixa Forum area, you will have passed by one of its main attractions: the Poble Espanyol. A visit to this miniature sample of Spanish architecture is highly recommended, not only for the appeal of its architectural diversity, but to call in at the many traditional craft shops where you'll be sure to find that special gift you've been looking for. It's so interesting that you may lose track of time, but don't worry, if hunger calls you're in the right

Calatrava Tower.

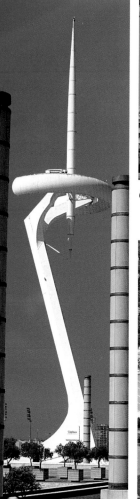

Caixa Forum Arts Centre.

Palau Sant Jordi (foreground) and Olympic Stadium.

MNAC and some examples of the works in its collection.

place to find a choice of restaurants offering a range of fine regional dishes.

Continuing your itinerary, the Palau Nacional or National Palace on Montjuïc was the visible symbol and most important building of the 1929 Exposition to which we have already referred. Set in the Plaça del Mirador, the building's façade is presided over by a great central dome, two smaller domes at either end and four towers in Compostela Gothic style. Inside, the oval-shaped main hall is on a grandiose scale, in a style that perfectly combines Classicist and Churrigueresque elements.

But the main attraction of the Palace is the Catalan National Museum of Art (MNAC), with a range of exhibition rooms displaying collections of Romanesque, Gothic, Renaissance and Baroque art of an incalculable value. In 2004 the Museum was enriched by the arrival of the collection of the Museum of Art of Catalonia in Ciutadela, and later, in 2005, it received a significant part of the Thyssen-Bornemisza collection from the Monastery of Pedralbes. The first of these included works by Catalan artists from the early 19th to the mid 20th centuries, and the second, pieces by masters

Grec Theatre.

like Fra Angelico, Titian, Ceruti, Canaletto and Rubens.

Cutting back across the mountain past the Olympic Ring to the Font del Gat fountain you come across the Ethnological Museum with its well-presented collection of pieces from indigenous peoples of Australia, Africa, Central and South America and some of the Pacific islands.

Lower down is a great stairway leading to a spacious gardened area and, as if concealed from prying eyes, the Greek Theatre, an open-air venue used for large events and theatrical works. With the mountain itself as a natural rocky backdrop and its semicircular shape calling to mind the theatres of Ancient Greece, the 'Grec', as it is popularly known by the Catalans, is a real gem. Although abandoned for some years, these days 'nights at the Grec' especially during the summer festival are now a tempting tourist and cultural attraction on Barcelona summer evenings.

Near the Grec Theatre is the Archaeological Museum, whose impeccable installations display an extensive collection of figures from cultures ranging from the Palaeolithic to the Visigothic periods in Catalonia and the Balearic Islands, including pieces of mosaic, pottery and sculptures from the Greek and Roman eras.

On your way down from your visit to the Palau Nacional you find the 'Font Lluminosa de Montjuïc' to give it its formal name, or the 'Font Màgica' or Magic Fountain as it is commonly known, a spectacle of col-

Archaeological Museum.

our, water, light and sound that literally defies description, and completely free. It's difficult to convey the appeal of the musical score combined with the water, light and colour of the fountain if you haven't experienced it for yourself. Add to this the illuminated Palace above, with its nine beams of light that seem to reach down from the sky, and the view over the nearby Plaça Espanya, with the profile of Tibidabo Mountain as a backdrop, the whole scene is quite sensational, especially if you can catch it at dusk.

Another pretty and less imposing but

MNAC and illuminated fountains.

Sculpture 'Dona i Ocell'.

Plaça de les Arenes.

equally interesting fountain, in the centre of Plaça Espanya, was a product of the ingeniousness of Josep M. Jujol. It consists of three large columns featuring several sculptural groups. If you reached the square along the Avinguda Reina Maria Cristina, you will have walked through the grounds of the Barcelona Trade Fair site, with its two high towers created by Ramón Raventós.

In its day, the Les Arenes bull ring on the Plaça witnessed impassioned afternoons with famous bull-fighters, but is now being redesigned and will shortly open as a new city leisure centre.

The last point of interest on this route is to be found in Carrer Tarragona just beyond the square, in the Parc de l'Escorxador park. This is the 22-metre high work of Joan Miró entitled 'Dona i Ocell' (Woman and Bird).

The Port and surrounding area

The maritime part of Barcelona was one of the areas that benefited most from the rush to improve infrastructures in 1992 in readiness for the Olympic Games. The Industrial Revolution had filled the area around the Port of Barcelona with factories, but thanks to work done for games, the city has now regenerated its maritime façade.

The city's port, divided into two areas, Port Vell (the Old Port) and Port Nou (the New Port), has been rehabilitated with great success. In fact, the Port Vell area

Some views of the port.

has become a delightful space open to the Mediterranean. After a browse in the small weekend collectibles market at Columbus, visitors can stroll over the the Rambla del Mar, a striking curvy new pedestrianised wooden walkway that links the esplanade at Columbus and the Rambla with Maremagnum, a bustling centre with leisure, shopping and eating facilities. In its 39,000 m2 you can enjoy lots of space and shops, restaurants, bars, terraces, mini golf and cinemas, with the plus of a visit to the Barcelona Aquarium. This is among the world's most important centres on Mediterranean habitats and one of the main facilities in Europe. The aquarium has an immense circular oceanarium which can be viewed under water through 80 metres of transparent tunnel. In its waters live 11,000 members of 450 different species of marine fauna, including several breeds of shark.

If you want to combine this with another spectacular visit, this time to the cinema, you have the Imax nearby, which uses three modern systems of large-scale projection: Imax, Omnimax and 3D.

The triangle formed by the end of the Ramblas, the monument to Columbus and Maremagnum has the special appeal of being a mixture of old Barcelona with

Fishing port.

Aquarium.

Pleasure boats.

Maremagnum. Shopping Centre, cinemas, a wide range of food and fun in general

Panoramic view of Maremagnum and the marina.

the fresh air of the new Mediterranean esplanade. You can discover some other hidden corners of the port by taking a short sea trip on board one of these Barcelona classics, the 'Golondrinas' pleasure boats which set sail from the esplanade.

Another interesting visit in the area is to the Museum of History of Catalonia, in the Barceloneta district, set in the tall Palau de Mar building nearby.

Not far away, overlooking the Maremagnum area and between the two boarding points for ferries to Mallorca rises the World Trade Centre, a business and shopping centre which itself resembles a large cruise ship! Just a bit further south is a great swing bridge inaugurated in 2001 and known as the Gate of Europe.

Leaving the Port Area, and going back to a recurrent theme in this guide - how the work done for the 1992 Olympics transformed the appearance of the city. This is particularly true in the area known as Poble Nou, a district which still had a great many old industrial buildings and factories in 1992. One of the great works of this period transformed this district's shoreline, turning it into what was to become one of the most exciting competition sites, the Olympic Port. This is now one of the most popular places with Barcelona residents and tourists alike, a favourite spot for spending a perfect weekend evening enjoying fine food in its restaurants, or swaying to the beat of the music in its discotheques at night.

In summer, the area's wide beaches offer impeccable facilities for bathers.

Two of the most striking sights in the Port are its large towers, the Mapfre Tower and the Hotel Arts. You can also try out your luck nearby, at Barcelona Casino.

Hotel Arts and the Mapfre Tower, with Marbella beach in the foreground.

Barcelona is justly known as the City of Festivals and Conferences, and in 2004 it widened its appeal by organising the Multicultural Forum of the Nations here. Land near the Port was earmarked for development and an area of 30 hectares was reserved for building the Forum, which has become one of the largest leisure and cultural amenities in the world. Some of the most outstanding structures are the Forum Building itself with its triangular shape, the Barcelona International Convention Centre (CCIB), which can accommodate 26,000 participants, and a brand new marina.

World Trade Center.

Palau del Mar, the building that hosts the Catalan Museum of History.

Forum.

Agbar Tower.

Not far from the Olympic Port is the National Theatre of Catalonia, the work of architect Ricardo Bofill, with three theatres of different sizes. Continuing past this to the Plaça de les Glòries Catalanes, you cannot miss the spectacular Agbar Tower, which apart from its stunning outline, can offer special lighting effects with the changing illumination of its tinted aluminium and transparent glass construction. At 142 metres high, the lookout point at the top of the building gives a breathtaking view over the whole city of Barcelona.

Index